Presidents' Day

by Laura Alden
illustrated by Joy Friedman

created by Wing Park Publishers

CHILDRENS PRESS ®
CHICAGO

Library of Congress Cataloging-in-Publication Data

Alden, Laura, 1955-
    Presidents' Day / by Laura Alden ; illustrated by Joy Friedman.
      p.   cm. — (Circle the year with holidays)
    "Created by Wing Park Publishers."
    ISBN 0-516-00691-6 (lib. bdg.)
    1. Presidents' Day — Juvenile literature.   [1. Presidents' Day. 2.
Washington, George, 1732-1799. 3. Lincoln, Abraham, 1809-1865.]
I. Friedman, Joy, ill. II. Title. III. Series.
E176.8.A43 1994
973′ .092′2—dc20
[B]   93-37095
                                                 CIP
                                               AC

Presidents' Day

Both Washington and Lincoln were born in the middle of February. We can easily celebrate both birthdays on Presidents' Day.

Both men have many places named after them. Each has a Memorial in Washington, D.C., our nation's capital.

If you go to Washington, be sure to visit the Washington Monument and the Lincoln Memorial.

"Yankee Doodle went to town riding on a pony," sang the children. "He stuck a feather in his cap and called it macaroni."

Carey didn't really feel like singing, even though it was Presidents' Day.

Carey was worried about the quiz they were going to have later. It was going to be on Presidents Washington and Lincoln.

Carey didn't really know why presidents were important. George Washington was the first one. Abraham Lincoln was the sixteenth one. That seemed to be about it.

"Presidents are the leaders of our country, the United States," said Carey's teacher, Ms. Clark. "Today we are celebrating the birthdays of our two most famous presidents. Does anyone know anything about them?"

Several children raised their hands. Carey looked out the window. She wondered whether the quiz would be hard.

The teacher handed out pictures of money. There was George Washington, the first president, on the one dollar bill.

There was Abraham Lincoln, the sixteenth president, on the five dollar bill.

"George Washington was a very brave soldier," said Ms. Clark. "He led our country in the fight to be free from England.

"Abraham Lincoln was brave, too. He kept the United States from splitting into two countries during the Civil War. He also decided that the slaves should be free people."

Carey thought presidents must have to work very hard. She wondered if they had to take quizzes when they were children.

"We're going to work on art projects now," said Ms. Clark.

The other children moved quickly to the art tables. "Walk!" called Ms. Clark. "Keep your hands and feet to yourself."

Carey didn't hear. She was thinking about the quiz.

"Carey?" said Ms. Clark. "Come on."

Suddenly there was a loud knock on the
classroom door.

"Come in," called Ms. Clark.

And in came George Washington and
Abraham Lincoln!

Carey stared at them. She knew they could
not really be the presidents, but they looked
just like them.

"Class, we have two very special guests today," said Ms. Clark. "Please say hello to President George Washington and President Abraham Lincoln."

"Hello," said all the children.

"Greetings!" said Washington, with a soldier salute.

"How are you children?" said Lincoln, with a nod.

"Children, do you have any questions for our two most famous presidents?" asked Ms. Clark.

Washington and Lincoln sat down and took off their hats.

Carey raised her hand. "When you were little, what was it like?"

23

George Washington smiled. "I grew up in a big house in Virginia," he said in a strong voice. "I rode horses and liked to hunt and fish. I liked numbers and making maps."

"I grew up in a log cabin," said Lincoln in
a quiet voice. "I loved books and telling
stories."

Carey walked up to Mr. Lincoln. "Did you have to work hard?" she asked.

"Yes, but I played hard, too," he said.

The other children gathered around, asking questions.

When they were done, Carey said, "Our class is celebrating your birthdays today."

"This is our way of thanking you for being good leaders of our country," said Ms. Clark.

"Happy birthday to you. Happy birthday to you," sang all the children.

Then they all joined in a Presidents' Day parade—with flags and hats and musical instruments. Carey beat the drum.

The presidents waved to all the children. The children waved right back.

Presidents' Day really was a special day. Carey had learned many interesting things about the presidents. Now she wouldn't mind taking that quiz. It would be a snap!

Activities

Presidents' Day Fun

You can have a lot of fun planning a birthday party for the presidents. You may want to serve cherry punch and cherry cupcakes. (You'll know why after you read about the legend of George Washington and the cherry tree on page 32.) What other foods will you have at your party?

Perhaps your class would like to invite two men to dress up as Washington and Lincoln and come to your party. You might like to make them birthday cards and sing "Happy Birthday" to them.

My Three-Cornered Hat

George Washington lived almost two hundred years ago. Clothing styles were very different then. Many people wore three-cornered hats. Here is a fun song about a hat with three corners:

> My hat it has three corners;
> Three corners has my hat.
> And had it not three corners,
> It would not be my hat.

Once you have learned the song, sing it again, but instead of singing the word "hat," make a triangle with your fingers over your head. The next time, instead of singing the word "three," hold up three fingers. The last time, instead of singing the word "corners," stick out one elbow. Try singing the song fast, using all three hand symbols. It's hard to do!

Lincoln's Log Cabin

You will need:
—a ½ pint milk carton   —scissors
—pretzel sticks   —glue
—peanut butter   —cotton ball
—butter knife   —stapler
—construction paper

1. For the roof of the cabin, cut out a piece of construction paper, 4½" x 3¼". Fold over top of carton (as pictured) and staple as shown.

2. Spread the sides of the carton with peanut butter (not too thick). Break the pretzels to the length you need and stick them onto the peanut butter.

3. Make a square chimney out of construction paper. Cut a "V" in the bottom of the chimney to make it fit on the top of the roof as shown. Glue in place. Glue a cotton ball on top of the chimney to look like a puff of smoke.

Presidents' Day Windsock

You will need:
—a large rectangle of tagboard   —stapler
  or heavy paper   —tape
—crayons, markers or paint   —string
—red, white, and blue crepe paper   —hole punch

1. Decorate the tagboard. You may want to draw the United States flag or pictures of presidents. Then roll the tagboard into a tube and staple it together.

2. Tape red, white, and blue streamers onto the bottom of the windsock. Punch three holes along the top edge of the windsock. Tie a piece of string about 5 inches long to each hole. Tie the other ends of the strings together.

The Legend of Washington and the Cherry Tree

A legend is a story told again and again through the ages. Some legends are only partly true, and some are not true at all. One popular legend about George Washington says that when he was a boy, he chopped down a beautiful cherry tree with his hatchet. His father was furious and asked who had chopped down the tree. George answered, "I cannot tell a lie, Father. I did it with my hatchet." Many now say this story might not have happened, but it's a story we tell to show the kind of person George Washington was—honest and brave. But perhaps the story really is true.

The True Story of Lincoln's Beard

Just before Abraham Lincoln was elected president in 1860, an 11-year-old girl named Grace Bedell wrote to him. She said she thought he would look better with a beard. Lincoln took her advice and wore a beard from then on.